The Evolution of Elegance.

Fashion Through the Ages: A detailed guide.
             by

Elizabeth Daniel.

Copyright © 2024 by Elizabeth Daniel.
All rights reserved.
No part of this book may be reproduced, stored in a retrieval system or transmitted in any form or by any means, electronic, mechanical, photocopying, recording or otherwise without the prior written permission of the copyright owner.
Printed in United States.
First Edition.

Acknowledgements.

I am grateful to:
- *The Omniscient God, the giver of Wisdom and Grace.*
- *My eldest brother, Michael Ozeh, for his unwavering support and firm belief in my dreams.*

- *My Fashion Coach, Auntie Charity, for her dedicated guidance and mentorship.*
- *My Readers around the world, for their enthusiasm and encouragement.*

Dedication.

Dedicated to:
God, who calleth forth those things which be not as though they were.

To Myself,
For believing in my dreams and turning them into reality.

Preface.

In the world of Fashion, Elegance cannot be overemphasized. It is the very essence of Dressing. From the intricate pleats of ancient Egyptian linens to the opulent courts of Renaissance Europe, Fashion has chronicled the aspirations, values and creativity of human civilization.

This book, "Evolution of Elegance" invites you on a fascinating journey through the ages exploring the transformative power of fashion and it's enduring impact on our culture, identity and beauty standards. Through the pages, we will delve into the historical tapestry, weaving together threads of art, technology and social change that have shaped the course of fashion. We'll witness the birth of iconic styles, the rise of legendary designers and the evolution of textiles from humble fibers to sumptuous fabrics.

Join me on this odyssey through the evolution of elegance as we uncover the stories, inspirations and innovations that have defined the art of fashion for centuries.

Table of Contents.
i) Acknowledgements
ii) Dedication
III) Preface
Chapter 1. Ancient Civilizations.
Chapter 2. The Renaissance to the Enlightenment.
Chapter 3. The Enlightenment and the Industrial revolution.
Chapter 4. The late 19th and early 20th centuries.
Chapter 5. The 1960s to the 1990s
Chapter 6. Contemporary fashion and beyond.

Chapter 1.
Ancient Civilizations.

The cradle of Fashion.

The origins of fashion can be traced back to ancient civilizations, where clothing and adornment were not only a reflection of personal style but also a symbol of status, power and cultural identity. In this chapter, we'll embark on a journey through the ancient world exploring the fashion highlights of Egypt (3050 BCE - 391 CE), Greece and Rome (8th Century BCE - 476 CE) and through to the middle ages.

Egypt.

The land of the Pharaohs.

Ancient Egyptian fashion was a testament to their advanced civilization. Linen garments, often pleated and draped, adorned the elite, while headdresses and symbolic jewelry signified power and spiritual connection.

Key Fashion Elements;

- Linen garments: pleated and draped, often worn with a schenti (loincloth)
- Headdresses: symbolic crowns, headcloths and nemes (striped cloth)
- Jewelry: Collars, pectorals and amulets featuring sacred symbols and deities.
- Footwear: Sandals and Papyrus shoes.

Iconic Looks;

- Pharaohs: pleated linen robes, nemes headdresses and symbolic jewelry.
- Nobility: draped garments, headcloths and ornate collars.
- Priests: Simple linen clothes, headcloths and amulets.

Greece.

The Birthplace of Democracy.

Ancient Greek fashion was characterized by simplicity, elegance and proportion. Draped garments, intricate pottery and ornate jewelry reflected their love of beauty and art.

Key Fashion Elements;

- Draped garments: Togas, himation and peplos (pleated robes)
- Fabric: Linen and wool, often embroidered or dyed.
- Jewelry: Wreaths, diadems and amulets featuring mythological motifs.
- Footwear: Sandals and lace-up boots.

Iconic Looks.

- Philosophers: Simple togas and himations often worn with a laurel wreath.
- Nobility: Ornate tops, diadems and intricate jewelry.
- Theater: Colorful costumes and masks for performance.

Rome.

The Eternal City.

Ancient Roman fashion was a fusion of Greek and Etruscan styles, with a focus on grandeur and luxury. Ornate garments, intricate jewelry and elaborate hairstyles reflected their power and sophistication.

Key Fashion Elements;

- Togas: White for citizens, purple for nobles, and red for Senators.
- Tunics: Long-sleeved and embroidered, often worn with a belt.
- Jewelry: Intricate necklaces, bracelets and earrings featuring gemstones.
- Footwear: Sandals, slippers and lace-up boots (calcei)

Iconic Looks:

- Senators: White togas with purple stripes, red shoes and laurel wreaths.

- Nobility: Ornate tunics, jewelry and hairstyles.
- Gladiators: Leather armor, helmets and sandals.

The Middle Ages.

A Time of Opulence.

Fashion during the middle ages was characterized by grandeur, luxury and religious influence. Elaborate garments, intricate embroidery and symbolic colors reflected the wearer's status, occupation and allegiance.

Key Fashion Elements;

- Robes: Long, flowing and often embroidered with religious symbols.
- Doublets: Close-fitting jackets, often worn with hose (tight-fitting pants).
- Headwear: Crowns, mitres (Bishop's hats) and hoods.
- Footwear: Pointed shoes, ankle boots and pattens (wooden soles)

Iconic Looks:

- Kings and Queens: Regal robes, crowns, and scepters.
- Nobility: Ornate doublets, hose and cloaks.
- Clergy: Simple robes, mitres, and crosses.

Chapter 2.
The Renaissance to the Enlightenment.

A Cultural Awakening.

The Renaissance marked a significant shift in fashion, as classical Greek and Roman style influenced clothing design. Luxurious fabrics, intricate details, and refined silhouettes characterized this era.

Key Fashion Elements:

- Gowns: flowing, with tight-fitting bodices and full skirts.
- Doublets: Close-fitting, often with puffed sleeves.
- Headwear: Hats, caps and hoods, adorned with feathers and jewels.

- Footwear: Pointed shoes, ankle boots, and chopines (platform shoes)

Iconic Looks:

- Royalty: Ornate gowns, doublets and regal headwear.
- Nobility: Elegant gowns, doublets and refined accessories.
- Artists: Simple, yet elegant attire, often with a cloak and hat.

The Baroque and Rococo Era.

Opulence and Extravagance.

This era was marked by extravagant fashion, with elaborate designs, rich fabrics and dramatic accessories. The rise of the middle class also led to a growth in fashion awareness and expression.

Key Fashion Elements:

- Gowns: Ornate, with intricate embroidery and beading.

- Coats: Long, with wide sleeves and ornate buttons.
- Headwear: Wigs, hats and hoods, adorned with feathers and jewels.
- Footwear: High heels, with intricate buckles and straps.

Iconic Looks:

- Royalty: Extravagant gowns, coats and wigs.
- Nobility: Ornate gowns, coats, and refined accessories.
- Emerging middle class: Simplified versions of aristocratic fashion.

Chapter 3.
The Enlightenment and the Industrial Revolution.

A new Era of Practicality.

As the Enlightenment emphasized reason and intellect, fashion shifted towards more practical and comfortable clothing. The Industrial Revolution introduced new textile technologies, and mass production, making fashion more accessible.

Key Fashion Elements:

- Dresses: Simplified, with fewer embellishments and a focus on comfort.
- Coats: Cutaway coats and tailcoats with a more streamlined silhouette.
- Headwear: Top hats, bonnets and caps.
- Footwear: Ankle boots and shoes with a more practical design.

Iconic Looks:

- Intellectuals: Simple, yet elegant attire, often with a top hat.
- Middle class: Practical dresses and coats, with a focus on durability.
- Working class: Simple, functional clothing, often with an apron.

Chapter 4.
The Gilded age.

A time of great change.

This era saw the rise of haute couture, the emergence of new fabrics and technologies and a growing emphasis on individuality and self-expression.

Key Fashion Elements:

- Dresses: Hourglass silhouettes, bustles and corsets.
- Coats: Tailcoats, overcoats and the emergence of the trench coat.
- Headwear: Top hats, bowlers and the rise of hats for women.
- Footwear: High heels, button boots and the introduction of sneakers.

Iconic Looks:

- Aristocracy: Opulent, custom-made clothing.
- Upper class: Elegant, refined attire.
- Emerging middle class: More affordable, ready-to-wear clothing.

The Roaring Twenties to the 1950s.

An Era of Glamour and Rebellion.

This period saw a significant shift in fashion, with the rise of Hollywood glamor, the flapper style and the emergence of Youth culture.

Key Fashion Elements:

- Dresses: Flapper styles, shift dresses, and the rise of Evening wear.
- Coats: Fur coats, trench coats, and the emergence of leather jackets.
- Headwear: Cloche hats, fedoras, and the rise of Sunglasses.
- Footwear: High heels, Mary Janes, and the introduction of sneakers.

Iconic Looks.

- Flappers: Short dresses, beads and a bobbed haircut.
- Hollywood stars: Glamorous evening wear and sophisticated suits.
- Youth Culture: Leather jackets, jeans and the emergence of casual wear.

Chapter 5.
The 1960s to the 1990s.

An Era of Counterculture and Grunge.

This period saw a significant shift in fashion, with the rise of counterculture, punk rock, and grunge. Fashion became more eclectic and individualistic.

Key Fashion Elements:

- Dresses: Mini dresses, maxi dresses and the rise of vintage clothing.
- Coats: Peacoats, denim jackets, and the emergence of leather trench coats.
- Headwear: Berets, headbands, and the rise of Baseball caps.
- Footwear: Go-go boots, platform shoes, and the introduction of sneakers as fashion statements.

Iconic Looks:

- Hippies: Bell-bottom jeans, tie-dye shirts and long hair.

- Punk Rockers: Ripped fishnets, leather jackets and spiked hair.
- Grunge Icons: Flannel shirts, ripped jeans and Doc Martens.

Chapter 6.
Contemporary Fashion and Beyond.

An Era of Sustainability and Self-expression.

Today, Fashion is more diverse and global than ever, with a growing focus on sustainability, body positivity, and personal style.

Key Fashion Elements:

- Dresses: Gender-neutral, eco-friendly and Versatile designs.
- Coats: Sustainable materials, oversized silhouettes and statement pieces.
- Headwear: Hats, hoodies and head scarves as fashion statements.
- Footwear: Sneakers, boots and shoes with a focus on comfort and sustainability.

Iconic Looks:

- Red-carpet: Glamorous, eco-friendly gowns and suits.
- Street style: Personalized, eclectic fashion with a focus on individuality.
- Influencers: Body-positive, sustainable fashion with a focus on self-expression.

Let's take a brief look at some of the World's Timeless Designers:

- **Coco Chanel: Little Black Dress, Chanel No. 5**
Coco Chanel is a pioneering French fashion designer who revolutionized women's fashion with her modernist and minimalist approach.

- **Christian Dior: New Look Collection, Bar Suit.**
Christian Dior, A French fashion designer who transformed the industry with his iconic "New Look" collection in 1947.

- **Yves Saint Laurent: Beatle Boot, Le Smoking Tuxedo.**

Yves Saint Laurent is a French fashion designer who popularized ready-to-wear fashion and was known for his beatnik and safari-inspired designs.

- **Vivienne Westwood: Punk Rock Styles, Corset Dress.**
Vivienne Westwood is a British fashion designer who was a key figure in the punk and new wave movements and is known for her bold and provocative designs.

- **Alexander McQueen: Armadillo Shoes, Skull Motif**
Alexander McQueen is a British fashion designer who was known for his dramatic and avant-garde designs that blended fashion and art.

-**Marc Jacobs.**
Marc Jacobs is an American fashion designer who is known for his grunge-inspired designs and his influence on street wear fashion.

-**Rei Kawakubo.**
Rei Kawakubo is a Japanese fashion designer who is known for her avant-garde and conceptual

designs that challenge traditional notions of beauty and fashion.

-Miuccia Prada.

Miuccia Prada is an Italian fashion designer who is known for her minimalist and intellectual approach to fashion and her use of bold colors and geometric shapes.

Other Iconic designers include:

- **Tom Ford.**

An American fashion designer who launched his eponymous brand in 2005, after working with Gucci and Yves Saint Laurent.

- **Stella McCartney.**

The daughter of Paul McCartney, English fashion designer who launched her eponymous line in 2001.

- **Tommy Hilfiger.**

An American designer known for his red, white and blue striped clothing, who was awarded the CFDA Menswear Designer of the Year award in 1995.

- **Ralph Rucci**

An American fashion designer who created the luxury fashion line, Chado Ralph Rucci.

- **Jean-Paul Gaultier**

A French fashion designer who worked with established fashion designer, Pierre Cardin, as his assistant and was working as the creative director for Hermès between 2003 and 2010.

- **Daphne Guinness.**

An English Socialite and Fashionista who began her career working with Isabella Blow and Karl Lagerfeld.

- **Donatella Versace.**

An Italian fashion designer, socialite, model and Businesswoman who inherited the Versace brand from her brother Gianni.

- **Diane von Furstenberg.**

A Belgian designer who launched the iconic wrap dress in 1974.

- **Jimmy Choo**

A Fashion designer from Malaysia who learnt the art of shoemaking from a young age.

- **John Varvatos**

An American Designer who began practicing his skills with Polo Ralph Lauren and Calvin Klein.

GLOSSARY.

- Toga: A traditional ancient Roman garment, a loose, draped fabric worn over the shoulder and around the body.

- Amulet: An ancient ornament worn to protect the wearer from harm or bring good fortune.

- Tunic: A basic garment in ancient Greece and Rome, a knee-length, sleeveless shirt.

- Schenti: An ancient Egyptian garment, a pleated skirt worn by both men and women.

- Wreaths: Circular arrangements of flowers, leaves, or other materials worn on the head or used as decoration.

- Peplos: A ancient Greek garment, a long, rectangular cloth wrapped around the body and pinned at the shoulder.

- Himation: A ancient Greek garment, a large, rectangular cloth wrapped around the body and over the shoulder.

- Ornate garments: Decorative clothing with intricate designs, patterns, and embellishments.

-Philosophy: A belief (or systems of beliefs) accepted as authoritative by some group or schools.

-Iconic: Relating to or having the characteristics of an icon.

-Fashion: The latest and most admired styles in clothes, cosmetics and behavior.

-Sneakers: A canvas shoe with a pliable rubber sole.

-Boots: Footwear that covers the whole foot and lower leg.

-Gown: A Woman's dress usually with a close-fitting bodice and a long flared skirt, often worn on formal occasions. (Today, gowns are taking various, beautiful shapes and styles more classy and more comfortable.)

-Jeans: Close-fitting trousers of heavy denim for manual work or casual wear. (Today, Jean wears are rocked to elaborate occasions like parties, and is no longer a casual wear. Jeans are now a trendy wear worn mostly by young people.)

-Royalty: Of a royal descent.

-Nobility: A privileged class holding hereditary titles.

-Headwear: Materials worn around or over the head.

-Extravagant: Unrestrained. Recklessly wasteful.

-Jewelry: An adornment (as a bracelet or ring or necklace) made of precious metals and set with gems.

-Bodice: Part of a dress above the waist.

-Clergy: A priest, Pastor or Prelate.

-Grandeur: The quality of being magnificent or splendid of grand.

-Luxury: Something that is an indulgence rather than a necessity.

-Bracelet: Jewelry worn around the wrist for decoration.

-Pharaoh: The title of the ancient Egyptian kings.

-Elite: A group or class of persons enjoying superior intellectual or social or economic ststatus.

-Renaissance: The period of European history at the close of the Middle Ages and the rise of the modern world. A cultural rebirth from the 14th through the middle of the 17th centuries.

-Tapestry: A heavy textile with a woven design; used for curtain and upholstery.

www.ingramcontent.com/pod-product-compliance
Lightning Source LLC
Chambersburg PA
CBHW071002220526
45471CB00007B/3143